Unmasking Emotional Abuse

Start the Healing

GREGORY L. JANTZ, PHD
WITH ANN MCMURRAY

Unmasking Emotional Abuse: Start the Healing
Copyright © 2020 Gregory L. Jantz
All rights reserved.
Rose Publishing, LLC
140 Summit Street
P.O. Box 3473
Peabody, Massachusetts 01961-3473
www.hendricksonrose.com

The information in this resource is intended as guidelines for healthy living. Please consult qualified medical, legal, pastoral, and psychological professionals regarding individual concerns.

All Scripture quotations, unless otherwise indicated, are taken from the Holy Bible, New International Version®, NIV®. Copyright ©1973, 1978, 1984, 2011 by Biblica, Inc.™ Used by permission of Zondervan. All rights reserved worldwide. www.zondervan.com The "NIV" and "New International Version" are trademarks registered in the United States Patent and Trademark Office by Biblica, Inc.™

Printed in the United States of America
010120VP

Contents

Unmasking Emotional Abuse

There is an old children's rhyme that says, "Sticks and stones may break my bones, but words will never hurt me."

And it's a lie.

Words can have a devastating impact. They cause people to believe the lies that are unfairly or unjustly spoken to them.

Emotional abuse is the intentional devaluing of one person by another in order to elevate themselves. Emotional abuse and its negative messages are false; they keep you from finding and understanding the truth of who you are. Emotional abuse takes different forms, but they all have the same destructive impact:

- It's the mother who yells in frustration at her son, "Why can't you be more like your sister?"

- It's the father who snorts in derision, "This girl will never amount to anything!"

- It's the sibling who regularly smirks, "Why would I want to be with you?"

- It's the husband who tells his wife, "You're too stupid to get a job!"

- It's the wife who tells her husband, "I could have done so much better than you!"

As you read through this book, remember this: Jesus said knowing the truth has the power to set you free.[1] As a child of God, the truth is that you were created to have emotional freedom, a strong sense of self, and a peace that surpasses understanding.[2] The good news is that what others may have sabotaged, God is able to rebuild.

Emotional abuse can come in the form of a one-time, traumatic event. However, it is more often perpetrated over time as a consistent pattern of one person treating another person unfairly and unjustly, while placing blame on the one being abused.

Through the years, I've seen more than I've wanted to of physical and sexual abuse. The most common form of abuse, though, is *emotional abuse*. While physical and sexual abuse are always accompanied by emotional abuse, the emotional abuse can also happen when neither physical nor sexual abuse is present. And, in the absence of those other forms of abuse, some people may doubt that true abusive behavior has taken place. After all, there is no black eye or bruising to see as evidence of an attack. The damage done, however, is real and devastating.

Some people were taught as children to "just get over it" or "move on" from harsh words or actions, but they weren't really told how to do that. Neither were they told how truly damaging those harsh words could be. So those children were left hurting, and years or decades later they feel embarrassed when they find themselves unable to just get over it and move on.

When I spoke with Jerry, he was deeply depressed. He'd had periods of depression through the years but had always been able to work himself out of them. This time was different. The only thing Jerry was now motivated to do was deny and run away from his life. The problem was, he knew that his life "wasn't so bad." Like most people, there were positives and negatives, but nothing so catastrophic that it would contribute to this utter sense of loss and hopelessness. He was ashamed because this time he couldn't "fix" himself.

"It's not like I was abused or anything . . ." Jerry said, and then proceeded to recount growing up with a mother too preoccupied to notice her son and a stepfather too estranged to offer any support. As we talked, Jerry often seemed embarrassed, fearful of making "too big a deal" out of what happened to him. Jerry had developed a survival strategy during childhood to minimize the pain from emotional abuse, believing if he told himself often enough it wasn't that bad, then it wouldn't be.

Pretending the pain didn't exist only lasted for so long. The older he got, the more difficult it was to run from the pain. The only way for him to heal was to deal with the pain head-on, facing it for what it was—the result of a persistent pattern of emotional abuse by the people who were supposed to love and support him. Over the years, Jerry fought hard to hold on to a childhood that wasn't real. But in order to get healthy, he needed to give up that illusion and come to grips with the reality that the words spoken to him back then did, indeed, hurt him. Once he acknowledged the pain, he was able to find a pathway to healing.

IF EMOTIONAL ABUSE CAN BE DIFFICULT TO ACKNOWLEDGE, THEN IT CAN ALSO BE DIFFICULT TO RECOGNIZE.

While physical and sexual abuse can be more visible and considered to be more severe, emotional abuse also has long-term and damaging effects. Because it isn't easily seen, it isn't easily acknowledged. And, if emotional abuse can be difficult to acknowledge, then it can also be difficult to recognize. How do you know what you remember was truly abusive? How do you know if a current relationship is an emotionally abusive one? Making this determination isn't always easy, because if you grew up with emotional abuse present, that abuse may have taken on a sense of normalcy. You didn't view what you experienced in the past as unusual or "wrong," so what's happening now seems normal.

You may not be the *best* judge where emotional abuse is concerned, but you are really the only judge. None of us have perfect relationships and all of us have experienced or engaged in saying or doing things in anger, frustration, fatigue, or just meanness. But if those things were part of a pattern, if they were used to belittle, devalue, shame, and ultimately control another person, they were abusive. Even if they were subtle or framed in a way that seemed helpful, "for your own good," they were still abusive. Those negative messages, often from people you looked to for love and guidance, become ingrained in who you are as a person. Removing them can seem like painfully peeling off parts of yourself, and this is a hard reality to face.

AS DIFFICULT AS IT IS TO ADMIT YOU'VE BEEN EMOTIONALLY ABUSED, IT MAY BE EVEN HARDER TO ADMIT THAT YOU'VE BEEN EMOTIONALLY ABUSIVE.

As difficult as it is to admit you've been emotionally abused, it may be even harder to admit that you've been emotionally abusive. The denial factor is significant. Sometimes, an abuser will be aware of what they are doing, but sometimes they won't, especially if the abuse seems normal to them. Tragically, as is often the case with other forms of abuse, emotional abusers may have a history of being abused themselves. Because the abuse is viewed as normal, it is perpetuated. This denial sets up an unacceptable cycle of being abused and then becoming abusive.

Signs *of* Emotional Abuse

The cycle of emotional abuse needs to be interrupted and stopped. The only way I know to do that is to learn how to recognize what emotional abuse truly is. Working with the damage caused by emotional abuse, I've identified the following consistent pattern of behaviors as emotionally abusive:

- Making the other person feel worthless

- Putting the blame for personal mistakes unfairly on the other person

- Minimizing the other person's point of view

- Threatening or hinting at physical or sexual harm

- Going into fits of rage and anger

- Making or implying promises with no intent to fulfill them

- Lying to avoid responsibility for attitudes, actions, or behaviors

- Refusing to acknowledge the other person's feelings

- Verbally or physically humiliating the other person through gestures, comments, or jokes

- Using false shame or guilt to manipulate the actions of the other person

- Not allowing the other person to articulate his or her feelings

- Denying the person access to personal possessions or pets

- Withholding appropriate financial resources

- Refusing to communicate with the other person—the silent treatment

- Displaying extreme ranges of mood

- Conditional agreements where the conditions keep changing to avoid fulfilling the agreement

- Using a hostile or sarcastic tone of voice with the other person

- Being critical of the other person's actions, thoughts, or remarks

- Viewing others as a part of the abuser's own personality, as opposed to separate individuals with a right to their own thoughts, actions, feelings, or opinions

- Belittling, humiliating, marginalizing, and/or ignoring the other person

RECOGNIZING A PROBLEM IS THE FIRST STEP IN SOLVING IT.

Coming to grips with emotional abuse is rarely easy, but recognizing a problem is the first step in solving it.

The Faces of Emotional Abuse

In this chapter, you will come face-to-face with the patterns—the "faces"—of emotional abuse. I've created names for each, to help you identify these patterns in people you know or even in yourself. You won't recognize every face, but I believe you'll recognize at least one. That face may be the face of a parent, a sibling, an extended family member, a spouse, a friend, a teacher, a pastor, or a coach. You may come to see one of those faces as the one that looks back at you in the mirror. While recognizing emotional abuse can be difficult, it is an essential step to healing.

■ ■ ■

THE COMMANDER-IN-CHIEF

Tom grew up in a family where his father was, without question, the man in charge. He controlled the lives of each family member with military precision. From the time the kids were awakened for school or chores to lights out in the evening, family members were expected to carry out their assigned duties and tasks with efficiency and proficiency. Slackers were not tolerated, with the sole definition of slacking determined by Tom's father.

Running the household as a tight ship, he avoided the messiness and inefficiency of shared decision-making. As second-in-charge, Tom's mother went along with and supported the program completely. Tom's life growing up took on a regimented regularity. Surprises were rare, as were laughter and spontaneity.

Tom and his siblings understood the rules. They followed what they could and conspired together to try and hide what they couldn't or wouldn't. When the rules weren't followed, punishments were meted out with great precision. The younger kids received so many whacks depending upon the offense. When they got older, privileges were withheld, not only for the initial offense but also until "trust" could be reestablished by proper behavior.

Punishments were expected but praise was not. Order was maintained but not affection. Anger, like slacking, was not tolerated. Tom remembered feeling part of a unit but rarely part of a family. Subsequently, he couldn't wait to get out of the house. Adulthood became the promise of finally getting to give the orders and have others obey.

Emotional abuse often takes forms meant to allow one person to control another, all the while denying that control is the ultimate objective. In a Commander-in-Chief, however, control is openly understood as the objective. The Commander-in-Chief does not attempt to hide the need for control.

> JESUS CALLED THEM TOGETHER AND SAID, "YOU KNOW THAT THE RULERS OF THE GENTILES LORD IT OVER THEM, AND THEIR HIGH OFFICIALS EXERCISE AUTHORITY OVER THEM. NOT SO WITH YOU. INSTEAD, WHOEVER WANTS TO BECOME GREAT AMONG YOU MUST BE YOUR SERVANT, AND WHOEVER WANTS TO BE FIRST MUST BE YOUR SLAVE—JUST AS THE SON OF MAN DID NOT COME TO BE SERVED, BUT TO SERVE, AND TO GIVE HIS LIFE AS A RANSOM FOR MANY."
>
> —Matthew 20:25-28

Phrases like these are heard often: "I said it and that settles it." "There is no room for discussion." "I'm the adult and you're not." "As long as you live under my roof, you do things my way." Pronouncements are given, not reasons.

A Commander-in-Chief may not be aware of the more subtle reasons for such a high need for control beyond, "I'm right and you're not." In some cases, a Commander-in-Chief may attempt to control other people in order to control their own fear, pain, embarrassment, or inadequacy. Commanders-in-Chief may say the control they demand is for "your own good," but in fact, it is for their own "good." When one person uses control to meet their own needs at the expense of another, that is emotionally abusive.

Going shopping with her mother was a nightmare for Jessie. She'd want to go to Old Navy, while her mother insisted they could find perfectly acceptable clothing at Sears. If Jessie wanted to try on a pair of black jeans, her mother would comment loudly enough for half the store to hear that jeans were meant to be blue and slacks were a much better option for school.

Each morning before school, Jessie tried to dash out the door before her mother took real notice. If she was unsuccessful, Jessie would stand and listen to her mother critique what she was wearing, how she was wearing it, what time she was leaving, how much makeup she had on, what she'd done with her hair that day, how she was getting to school, and what she was doing after school. Nothing was too small for her mother to notice and comment on.

Flying under the radar was impossible because Jessie's mother had an opinion about everything. And that everything didn't just encompass Jessie; everything meant everything. If they were out, everything could mean the demeanor of the clerk at the store, the way the person three cars ahead drove, the veracity of the discussion on the radio. Closer to home, it could be the volume on the television, the temperature of the room, the position of the chair, the setting on the light. All her life, Jessie lived under the stifling fog of her mother's opinions and critical nature.

With her mother's mind so full of her own opinions, Jessie learned the futility of attempting to express any of hers. She learned the definition of a "discussion" was an opportunity for her mother to fully explain herself to Jessie, sometimes in excruciating detail. Jessie still had her own opinions, but they were often at odds with her mother's. Over time, Jessie began to doubt herself, second-guessing decisions even when her mother was nowhere near. Of course, Jessie's mother was never truly absent because Jessie constantly heard that voice in her head wherever she went.

> FOOLS FIND NO PLEASURE IN UNDERSTANDING BUT DELIGHT IN AIRING THEIR OWN OPINIONS.
>
> —Proverbs 18:2

A sign I once saw read, "Everyone is entitled to their own opinion as long as it agrees with mine." This sign was meant to be funny, but for an Overbearing Opinion, that sign isn't a joke but a serious life statement.

The Overbearing Opinion has a way of sucking all the discussion out of a room, suffocating the opinions of others.

Healthy discussion allows for a variety of opinions to be expressed. Opinions are generally formed out of knowledge, personal experience, and the feelings those generate. Because of this, opinions can be intimate and unique reflections of those who express them. When opinions are not elicited, desired, or recognized, the person who espouses them is devalued.

The Overbearing Opinion does not view his or her opinion as an opinion; rather, he or she views that "opinion" as an incontrovertible fact. In this scenario, opinions may be challenged but facts must be accepted. The Overbearing Opinion seeks to quash discussion or disagreement in order to gain compliance, which is another word for control. This disregard for the opinions and feelings of others is emotionally abusive.

THE VENTAHOLIC

Something was going on with Logan. This happy, active second grader was suddenly making excuses for not going to school. His stomach hurt; he was too tired; his head hurt. Naturally, Logan's mother took him to his pediatrician. "There's nothing physically wrong with Logan," Amanda was told. "Something else is going on."

"Tell me about school," she asked Logan, attempting to pinpoint the problem. Immediately Logan tensed up, fidgeting in agitation.

"What's your favorite part of school?" she asked, trying a different tactic. He promptly replied, "Recess," which really wasn't much of a surprise.

"How are the other kids at school?" she tried. Logan started into an animated explanation of the kids he liked to play with and what they did together at recess. Amanda wondered about Logan being bullied, but that didn't seem to be the case, at least not at recess.

"Why don't you want to go school?" she finally asked outright. Logan hemmed and hawed and mumbled he just didn't want to go.

"But you have to go to school," Amanda patiently explained. "Besides, Mrs. Palmer says you're one of her best students." At the name of Mrs. Palmer, Logan sharply looked away.

"Is there something wrong with Mrs. Palmer?" Amanda asked.

Logan quickly said, "No, she's my teacher."

"I know she's your teacher, Logan, but do you like her?" Amanda thought she was finally getting somewhere.

"She yells a lot," Logan said by way of explanation.

"She yells a lot," Amanda repeated, thinking back over the times she'd volunteered in the classroom. "Well, she did raise her voice when I was there last week, but it was pretty noisy at the time."

"She's much louder when you're not there," Logan told her confidently. "She yells at everybody, even if they're not doing anything." His statement left Amanda at a loss, conflicted about what she was going to do. As she was thinking, Logan asked, "Why does she yell so much?"

If you were in a store and saw someone beat or hit a child, I would hope you would rush in to intervene. But it's different when the child receives a verbal beating. A part of you wants to stand up for the child because, surely, no one deserves to be spoken to that way. Another part of you recognizes this really isn't your business and you're supposed to stay out of it. Still, it's uncomfortable for the observer and humiliating for the child. You find yourself wondering, "What is going on with the adult?"

As a parent, there have been times when I've gone overboard with my verbal correction. Frustration, anger, fatigue, or exasperation can overwhelm just about anyone. But these lapses are few and far between, and immediately recognized as over the top.

> BUT NOW YOU MUST ALSO RID YOURSELF OF ALL SUCH THINGS AS THESE:
> ANGER, RAGE, MALICE, SLANDER, AND FILTHY LANGUAGE FROM YOUR LIPS.
>
> —Colossians 3:8

The Ventaholic is different. There is a pattern of heated, verbal rants. Once started, these rants don't seem to diminish; they seem to gather steam. Innocuous incidents can set them off because that person is like a volcano, boiling inside with the ongoing pressures of life. When those pressures are triggered, out spews a caustic verbal tirade less about what's just happened on the outside and more about what's fighting to escape on the inside.

While many of us succumb to this kind of venting on rare occasions, anger becomes a default setting for that person, with the internal filter always pointed toward life as unfair, unreasonable, or unjust. When enraged, the Ventaholic feels vindicated, powerful, invincible, and in control. Life has robbed them of whatever they feel they lack. They will angrily demand restitution from just about anyone, including those closest to them. In the rush of adrenaline, the Ventaholic may experience a rant as a form of physical pleasure, which can become addictive. Treating others as verbal punching bags is a classic sign of emotional abuse.

THE ALWAYS RIGHT

"*I* told you so," Mark's father said without looking up from the paper. "I told you that car wasn't worth anything. Don't expect me to help you with the repairs. You wanted it; it's your problem."

Mark had to admit all that was true. His father had warned him about the car. But did he have to be so smug about it? Mark could hear the satisfaction in his father's voice. Instead of being concerned about the fuel pump going out, he almost sounded happy; happy that, once again, he was proven right.

Mark couldn't count the times his father had said "I told you so" over the years. Just once, Mark wanted to be right about something, and not just right, but right at the same time his father was wrong. That was one of the reasons he'd overlooked some of the issues with the car. Sure, he'd known the car wasn't perfect, but the more his dad had talked it down, the more Mark felt the need to champion his selection.

If the fuel pump hadn't gone out, his dad would have found some other reason to declare "I told you so" where the car was concerned. Mark felt like his dad was just waiting, ready to pounce on any reason to stick it to him, to show he was right and Mark was wrong. Mark had stopped trying to figure out why he did that. As much as he wanted his father's approval, he knew he wasn't going to get it. Well, he couldn't figure out a way to fix the relationship, but he'd find a way to fix the car, without any help from his dad.

The Always Right can seem very similar to the Overbearing Opinion, but there is a distinction. While the Overbearing Opinion makes comments about everything, the Always Right waits and bides their time.

> FOR BY THE GRACE GIVEN ME I SAY TO EVERY ONE OF YOU: DO NOT THINK OF YOURSELF MORE HIGHLY THAN YOU OUGHT, BUT RATHER THINK OF YOURSELF WITH SOBER JUDGMENT, IN ACCORDANCE WITH THE FAITH GOD HAS DISTRIBUTED TO EACH OF YOU.
>
> —Romans 12:3

They are selective, searching for opportunities to not only prove they are right but also that the other person is wrong.

Generally, the person who is Always Right appears to be in competition with others. I've seen it with a sibling who competes with another sibling and with a parent who competes with a child. I've also seen it in the workplace, where a supervisor will target an employee.

Competitiveness is triggered in the relationship when the Always Right feels threatened by the other person.

Living with someone who is Always Right can be extraordinarily frustrating. If there's a difference of opinion and you're proven right, then the Always Right will shrug that situation off, as if it's not really that important. However, if you're proven wrong, you hear about it early and often. Because of the difficulty of dealing with someone who is Always Right, you may disregard your own decisions and just go with what the other person wants to do. When that happens, the other person gains control of the relationship and is able to perpetuate their emotional abuse.

THE INTIMIDATOR

- "If you tell Mom, I'll say it was your idea."

- "If you don't play the game our way, you can just leave."

- "If you don't get to bed right now, there'll be no computer for a week."

- "If you don't go along with these audit figures, you can look for another job."

- "If you don't do what I want, I'll leave."

- "If you don't, then . . ."

An Intimidator asserts control through issuing threats. Sometimes those threats are issued at the top of their lungs and other times they are conveyed through a whisper. Whether up-front or veiled, the threat is understood.

Generally, there are two types of Intimidators. The first type is all wind but no substance. They issue dire proclamations of what they are going to do but never seem to get around to doing it. A classic example of this is the parent who says, "I'm going to count to three!" This is followed by "I mean it—you've got to the count of three!" This becomes a type of game, with the child refusing to obey just to see how long it's going to take to push the parent over the edge.

> HIS MOUTH IS FULL OF LIES AND THREATS; TROUBLE AND EVIL ARE UNDER HIS TONGUE.
>
> —Psalm 10:7

This puts the child clearly in charge of the action. He or she may finally do what the parent wants, but not before initially controlling the parent. Now over the edge, that parent may strike out in anger and frustration, choosing consequences that are more severe than the initial situation warranted. The threat is elevated and carried out, but the encounter becomes an unhealthy contest of wills without a winner.

The other type of Intimidator is one who means every word they say and back it up with action. These are the type of people that others fear—at home, at school, or in the workplace.

> THEY SCOFF, AND SPEAK WITH MALICE; WITH ARROGANCE THEY THREATEN OPPRESSION.
>
> —Psalm 73:8

Whether the consequences the Intimidator chooses are expressed up front or arrived at out of frustration, they are always more severe than the situation warrants, which breeds resentment, bitterness, and anger. A person who physically threatens another is abusive. And, a person who verbally threatens another is also abusive.

THE JUDGE AND JURY

Lisa was court-ordered to go into counseling after shoplifting at several local department stores. She wasn't thrilled with the decision and made her displeasure known. She was tired of other people telling her what to do. By "other people" she meant adults, and specifically her parents.

I decided to do something unexpected and give her permission to leave my office. I told her, "If you don't want to be here, you can go." She looked shocked and asked what would happen with the court. I told her I didn't know, but I couldn't see any value in her staying if she didn't want to be there. She almost left: I could see her thinking it over; but she, almost defiantly, decided to stay.

Lisa grew up in a family dominated by her father. If her mother gave permission for her to spend the night at a friend's house but her father didn't approve, it didn't happen. The whole family could decide to go out to dinner, but if at the last minute her father was too tired, nobody went. If he didn't like a new piece of clothing or shoes, back it went to the store. There was no discussion. His decisions were final.

As Lisa got older, she came to realize that her father's decisions had more to do with how he was feeling at the time than anything else. In a good mood, he could be generous. But, if he was in a bad mood, there was no point in even asking; the answer would be no. So, Lisa stopped asking and started taking matters into her own hands.

She hid her activities from her parents, choosing to work through friends to get what she wanted. That's how the shoplifting happened. Lisa and a friend decided it would be easier to lift the clothes they wanted than go through either the hassle or the futility of asking their parents. Seemed like a good idea at the time, until mall security caught up with them.

> DO NOTHING OUT OF SELFISH AMBITION OR VAIN CONCEIT. RATHER, IN HUMILITY VALUE OTHERS ABOVE YOURSELVES, NOT LOOKING TO YOUR OWN INTERESTS BUT EACH OF YOU TO THE INTERESTS OF THE OTHERS.
>
> —Philippians 2:3-4

There is an incongruous instability to a Judge and Jury because often, the person doesn't just administer the law, they change it. What was perfectly acceptable on a Wednesday might not be on that Friday. A Judge and Jury is only concerned with the outcome of the decision, which is what they want to happen at any given time. The only consistency is their inconsistency. This inconsistency prevents another person from having the stability and surety of a healthy relationship. A person who lives under this system never knows from day to day what to anticipate, except disappointment. Sometimes, like Lisa, they find a way to create certainty by making and hiding their own decisions.

THE ROLLER COASTER

"*Whose* turn is it?" was always the question on a Saturday morning growing up. The kids would gather at the top of the stairs and huddle before deciding who would make the journey downstairs and report back. Sharon dreaded when it would be her turn.

The job, she explained, was to go downstairs and see what sort of mood Mom was in that day. If she was in a good mood, Sharon would run upstairs to report to the rest of the kids that the coast was clear. Mom in a good mood meant the kids could relax. They might even get to go to a friend's house or have someone over. Mom in a bad mood meant do what you're told, don't argue, don't ask for anything special, and don't get in her way. A bad mood meant more chores and stricter standards, leaving less time for play.

Her mother's good moods were like a cool breeze on a hot day—short and sweet. Bad moods generally lasted longer and had to be weathered like a storm. At almost fifty, Sharon still seemed perplexed about why her mother swung to such extremes. Sometimes, the kids were clearly at fault, but other times, Sharon couldn't remember anything they'd done to trigger the storm. She clearly loved her mother but still approached her with extreme caution, ever watchful when they were together to see which way the wind was blowing.

Roller coasters are huge attractions for a reason; they can be unbelievably exhilarating. You know as you're ratcheting up the incline that, before long, you'll be hurtled down and around and over and through. You also know that, at the end of it all, you'll arrive safely at the smooth stretch, wind-blown, red-faced, laughing, and catching your breath.

But, what if you never get to a smooth stretch? How would you feel if there was no getting off the roller coaster? Sharon spent her childhood strapped inside the roller coaster of her mother's moods, never knowing which way the ride was going to go next. School was safe. Friends were safe. Outside was safe. Home was not safe. Decades after leaving and establishing a home of her own, Sharon still felt that loss.

> LIKE A CITY WHOSE WALLS
> ARE BROKEN THROUGH
> IS A PERSON WHO LACKS
> SELF-CONTROL.
>
> —Proverbs 25:28

Emotions are not flatlined. They are meant to move up and down as each of us reacts to our circumstances. Healthy emotional regulation allows us to monitor our moods and moderate them, for our benefit and the benefit of others. Roller Coaster people do not regulate their emotions. Granted, there are some people who are unable to regulate their emotions due to physical conditions. Yet, I have found that Roller Coasters often make a choice not to regulate their emotions. Generally, if they feel it, they express it, regardless of how that emotion comes across, especially with family members. The intensity and the unchecked nature of uncontrolled emotions end up creating a pattern of emotional abuse.

THE PUT-DOWN ARTIST

"*What?* They actually hired you?" Jim's brother, Aaron, sounded incredulous. "Why would they do that?" he asked, as he rummaged through the pantry looking for something to eat. Jim could feel the familiar knot of anger twist in his stomach. Bad luck that Aaron had come into the room right when Jim was telling his friend, Mike, the news. Jim had been excited to get the job and now Aaron was making him pay.

"Great, now all my friends can watch my little brother make burgers." Aaron laughed and grabbed a bag of chips. "'Do you want fries with that?'" he mimicked in a nasal voice, shaking the bag. "What a joke!"

"It's not a joke," Jim spat back. "It's a job!" What he wanted to say, but didn't, was at least he had a job.

> IF AN ENEMY WERE INSULTING ME, I COULD ENDURE IT; IF A FOE WERE RISING AGAINST ME, I COULD HIDE. BUT IT IS YOU, A MAN LIKE MYSELF, MY COMPANION, MY CLOSE FRIEND, WITH WHOM I ONCE ENJOYED SWEET FELLOWSHIP AT THE HOUSE OF GOD, AS WE WALKED ABOUT AMONG THE WORSHIPERS.
>
> –Psalm 55:12-14

"Yeah, well, we'll see how long you keep it. Sometimes they hire a bunch of people and then get rid of the ones they don't like. Just because you got hired doesn't mean they'll like you." Aaron, as usual, seemed determined to undermine anything positive that came Jim's way.

When he'd talked to Mike, Jim was excited. Now, after listening to Aaron, he just felt nervous. What if he didn't keep the job? Aaron would never let him live it down.

> DO NOT LET ANY UNWHOLESOME TALK COME OUT OF YOUR MOUTHS, BUT ONLY WHAT IS HELPFUL FOR BUILDING OTHERS UP ACCORDING TO THEIR NEEDS, THAT IT MAY BENEFIT THOSE WHO LISTEN.
>
> –Ephesians 4:29

A Put-Down Artist uses words and tone of voice to degrade the value of another person. By employing this method, they seek to bring themselves up by pushing others down. I've found the worse the Put-Down Artist feels about him- or herself, the worse the verbal put-downs become. They can happen at any time, over anything. On that specific day, Aaron put down Jim for getting an entry-level job at a nearby fast food restaurant. However, prior to that, Jim suffered a chronic pattern of verbal put-downs from an older brother he longed to look up to.

Living with a Put-Down Artist can cause a person to develop a very thin skin. They might interpret someone's throwaway remark, casual comment, or misunderstood thought as one more personal assault. Their intense reaction to misinterpreted hostility and suspicion can cause undue stress in dealing with others. A thin skin complicates the formation and maintenance of relationships.

THE JEKYLL AND HYDE

Connie lived a double life. There was a Public Connie and a Private Connie. Public Connie was pleasant and competent. She was never rude, but she wasn't overly friendly. Public Connie appeared to have everything together. Privately, though, Connie was falling apart. Increasingly, she lived in fear that the messed-up, out-of-control Private Connie would show up in a very public setting. Secrecy needed to be maintained at all costs.

Growing up, Connie learned the necessity of maintaining secrets, creating a barrier between what was "public" and what was "private." Connie had grown up in a strict Christian home, attending church "whenever the doors were open." Both of her parents were leaders at the church and the entire family was expected to maintain that status.

"Sunday best" became more than clothing. Connie remembered learning to put on a smile as soon as she got out of the car, even though her father had yelled the entire way to church. She remembered watching her mother be patient with the children in her Sunday school class, knowing if she behaved similarly at home, there'd be hell to pay. She remembered standing in the foyer, being praised for something she'd done in school, still smarting over the harsh critique at home over the same thing.

Connie learned that she was on display in public and expected to put in a command performance every time. She was not allowed to be whiny, needy, angry, hungry, tired, or moody in public. Instead, she was to patiently wait for the show to be over.

Appearance was paramount. She learned not to do anything to expose the private aspects of her life and her family, ever. Before there were video games, Connie learned how to create a perfect avatar of herself that conducted her public life. The older she got, however, the harder it was to maintain that image, as the private pain and chaos kept leaking out in unexpected ways and places.

All of us tend to wear different "hats" in life. I'm a son, a brother, a husband, a father, a counselor, a business owner, a church leader, a friend, a mentor. I can have different moods and approaches depending upon which hat I'm wearing. Such is the flexibility of life.

The danger comes when I try to deny that I'm capable of the spectrum of human emotions and place a high value on appearing perfect. The further danger comes when, because I've polished my perfect public image, I feel justified in maintaining a less-than-perfect private persona.

TRUTH ALWAYS FINDS ITS WAY TO THE TOP.

Living with a Jekyll and Hyde means knowing the truth but being forbidden to acknowledge it. Because the false image is bright and shiny, the truth can seem tarnished and dirty, something that should be hidden and shameful. This is an upside-down world where lies are good and truth is bad.

Truth always finds its way to the top. While it may stay hidden for years, even decades, there comes a point when the effects of the truth are visible. Those visible effects lead to uncovering the hidden truth. The truth is that no one is perfect, and it is a lie to pretend otherwise.

THE STAND-UP COMIC

"*Julie's* such an airhead, it's amazing she doesn't just float away!"

"Carl, in accounting, he's smart about some things but really dumb about others. He spent so much time working on his presentation, he was late for it!"

"I heard Tracy bragging about her raise. The only thing she's really good at is taking her breaks."

"Did you hear Mike try to talk about the game last night? He doesn't know anything about football! He thinks a quarterback is a refund."

A Stand-Up Comic tries to keep everyone laughing, except for the butt of the joke. A Stand-Up Comic doesn't laugh with you but at you, using sarcasm, hyperbole, and exaggeration to beat down your self-image. Like a Put-Down Artist, a Stand-Up Comic uses verbal jabs to deflate and hurt people, but those jabs are wrapped in a joke. If you take offense, well, what's your problem? Can't you take a joke?

If you can't, then you're at fault, not the Stand-Up Comic. Instead of him or her being insensitive, you're being overly sensitive. The insult presented as a joke

44

provides the Stand-Up Comic with a tailor-made escape from blame.

There's nothing funny about being the punch line for someone else's joke. A Stand-Up Comic doesn't care about your feelings. What matters is gaining a laugh at your expense. In this way, they are seen as smart, funny, witty, or clever, while you're seen as incompetent, ridiculous, or clueless. This is a way for them to elevate themselves on the back of someone else and get other people to applaud them for it.

> LIKE A MANIAC SHOOTING FLAMING ARROWS OF DEATH IS ONE WHO DECEIVES THEIR NEIGHBOR AND SAYS, "I WAS ONLY JOKING!"
> —Proverbs 26:18-19

Over time, you may come to see yourself in a negative light because of the reaction of others. Or, you may try to beat the Stand-Up Comic by making a joke out of yourself. Better the class clown than someone else's punch line, right? Either way, you begin to view yourself as someone who cannot be taken seriously or respected.

"*Steve's* a great guy!" Paula smiled, allowing the nodding of her head to convey agreement. There were times when that certainly seemed true. The other times were what kept her from wholehearted endorsement.

Undeniably, Steve was a real charmer; Paula had come under his spell herself. When they'd first met, Paula found him romantic and funny and larger-than-life. When they were together, she felt special and a little surprised that Steve had chosen her. As soon as they'd moved in together, though, things changed. In public, he was caring and attentive. In private, he could be moody, isolating, and sometimes mean. Paula kept hoping he'd snap out of whatever funk he was in. But then she noticed that Steve could change quickly, particularly if someone else was around.

When she finally got up enough courage to talk to Steve about his behavior, he acted as if he had no idea what she was talking about. He acted wounded and astonished that she would say such terrible things about him. For every instance she brought up, he deflected with a reason or an excuse. Sometimes, he would just deny the whole thing ever happened that way and would accuse her of being negative toward him. He was so good at twisting what she remembered and putting her on the defensive for even bringing it up that Paula began to doubt what she remembered. She wasn't sure what was real anymore. Maybe it was really her fault. Maybe she was to blame for seeing things that way.

Illusionists are usually very good with words. They are good with their own words: defining, defending, excusing, explaining. They are good with the words of others: bending them, shaping them, twisting them around. After going three rounds with an Illusionist, you're not sure which end is up. If you are in a relationship with an Illusionist, you start to doubt your judgment, which is the point. Once you doubt your own judgment, the Illusionist is in a better position to force you to adopt his or hers.

> A FALSE WITNESS WILL NOT GO UNPUNISHED, AND WHOEVER POURS OUT LIES WILL NOT GO FREE.
>
> —Proverbs 19:5

Breaking away from an Illusionist can be extremely difficult, because to everyone else, "Steve's a great guy!" Other people don't know your truth and when you articulate that truth, you begin to look like the bad guy. Friends, even family, may place blame for problems on you. The Illusionist may provide his or her own reasons and rationales for why you're acting the way you are, none of which put you in a good light or are based on the truth. And, the more you insist upon telling the truth, the more you are called into question. The experience is like living in a world where everything is backward from the way it should be.

THE GUILT SHIFTER

When I first met Melissa, she couldn't have weighed more than eighty pounds. Pencil thin from anorexia, her skin was waxy, her pale face stark with protruding bones. At eighty pounds, Melissa was convinced she weighed much more. I soon came to learn that the extra weight Melissa was convinced she carried was guilt.

It was Melissa's fault that her mother gave up a promising dance career on the East Coast to get married. Her mother had gained fifty pounds while pregnant and it was Melissa's fault she'd never been able to get it off. When Melissa's father left, it was her fault; the marriage had been fine before Melissa entered the picture. Having to care for Melissa by herself meant that her mother could never realize her dream of establishing a dance studio. It was Melissa's fault that her talent languished and went unrecognized.

The blame for everything wrong with her mother's life was placed squarely on Melissa from an early age. In an odd way, Melissa's mother turned her into a warped confidant, explaining in unfiltered detail how Melissa's birth had ruined the life that should have been. In a desperate attempt to make up for her sins, Melissa did

49

everything she could to become a dancer herself. She became convinced losing more weight would gain her more talent.

By the time I met Melissa, she could barely walk up a set of stairs, let alone dance. Totally convinced of her worthlessness, Melissa determined that her mother's life would be so much better without her. The truth, unfortunately, was just the opposite. As a Guilt Shifter, Melissa's mother needed Melissa. The fact is that Melissa had become the most important person in her mother's world. Without Melissa, where would her mother place all her blame? Melissa had become the depository for her mother's resentment, bitterness, anger, and even envy.

TRUE GUILT IS A GOD-GIVEN BLESSING; ONE MEANT TO MOTIVATE CHANGED BEHAVIOR AND ELICIT APPROPRIATE REMORSE FOR WRONG ACTIONS.

For Guilt Shifters, the most important person is the one to whom they can shift blame. Without that person, Guilt Shifters would become responsible for their own decisions and failures. Such a burden is viewed as too great, so another, more vulnerable person is chosen to bear the guilt.

As they watch the other person strangle on all that guilt, they can feel a perverted sense of satisfaction. After all, they think, you're responsible for their pain, so why shouldn't you feel pain yourself? If you are responsible for their pain, then they should have the right to tell you what and how much you need to do to make up for it. Melissa's mother not only withheld emotional nourishment from her daughter, she demanded that Melissa feed her. Through anorexia, Melissa found a way to turn emotional starvation into physical starvation.

> ACQUITTING THE GUILTY AND CONDEMNING THE INNOCENT—THE LORD DETESTS THEM BOTH.
>
> —Proverbs 17:15

True guilt is a God-given blessing; one meant to motivate changed behavior and elicit appropriate remorse for wrong actions. Guilt Shifters, though, know nothing of true guilt because they avoid it themselves. Instead, they rely on false guilt, manufacturing whatever reasons are needed to keep the other person in line and willing to accept the burden of guilt. Once weighed down with guilt, the other person is much easier to control.

THE PLAYER OF FAVORITES

Chelsea took a break from warming up and scanned the bleachers one more time. She could see her mother dutifully sitting up with the other parents, but no sign of her father. Why did she always do this to herself? Why did she get her hopes up that, this time, maybe, he'd come to watch one of her track meets? Breathing deeply, she could feel the anger well up inside her. Good, she could use that on the track today. She felt angry, but also like crying. Her father could find a way to get to her brother's games but not her meets, like track wasn't a real sport but football and baseball were. She trained just as hard, maybe even harder. It was so unfair.

Chelsea had come to the tough conclusion several years ago that her dad loved her brother more than her. Oh, she knew he loved her too, but he clearly loved her brother in a different way. He was close to her brother and distant with her. He seemed to lump her in with her mother and treat her with casual, benign interest. Her father was interested in what she was doing, but he was excited by what her brother did. She could hear it in his voice and see it in his expressions and gestures. Just once, she'd love to see him respond to her that way.

She kept trying to find something that would attract his notice. She was good at track, very good, but he was never there to see it. No matter how many times she crossed the finish line, she could never seem to win the prize she wanted.

One of the most emotionally damaging conditions for a child is when a parent favors one child over another. In certain situations, a parent may treat all the children with the same low level of concern. But partiality is, in some ways, much worse for the child. If the parent treats all the children poorly, then they are all in the same boat. But, when a parent chooses one child over the other, the left-out child becomes a witness to that unattainable love and care. The child sees the love given to others, can watch it unfold from afar, but can't reach it. Usually, the child is left with only one conclusion—"I'm not worthy of that love."

> HE WOULD SURELY CALL YOU TO ACCOUNT IF YOU SECRETLY SHOWED PARTIALITY.
> —Job 13:10

There are complex reasons why a parent might gravitate more toward one child than another. Personalities come into play, as does temperament. Gender can certainly be a factor. Sometimes a child who is too much like a parent just naturally butts heads with them. Or, parent and child can be so much alike they form an immediate bond that isn't easily shared.

This conundrum of partiality is as old as Jacob and Esau from the Bible. Isaac, the father, preferred Esau, while Rebekah, the mother, preferred Jacob. This disparity in affection resulted in strife between Isaac and Rebekah, as well as between Esau and Jacob.[3] Playing favorites tears families apart.

THE PREACHER

Mark could feel it coming. Depending upon how his mom's day was going, it could be anywhere from five minutes to half an hour. If he could have forged her signature on the progress report, he would have done it. But she kept up with all the school stuff and knew a progress report was coming. Might was well get it over with.

Slouching over the counter wasn't an option when they were engaged in the "serious business" of his school progress, so he kept his back straight and his eyes straight ahead, waiting for her to read over the report. She'd read it once and was now going back over all the little comments. That wasn't a good sign. Mark figured she was gathering up ammunition to blast him. He wasn't wrong.

> HE HAS SHOWN YOU, O MORTAL, WHAT IS GOOD. AND WHAT DOES THE LORD REQUIRE OF YOU? TO ACT JUSTLY AND TO LOVE MERCY AND TO WALK HUMBLY WITH YOUR GOD.
>
> —Micah 6:8

Mark had to give her credit; she could blast with the best of them. The positive information got passed over without a comment.

Anything negative was proof positive he wasn't trying hard enough. She even brought up his aging grandparents and how disappointed they would be with his midyear science grade. They lived in Des Moines and he saw them twice a year.

Fifteen minutes later, the sermon was over. She'd laid out her case for condemnation and specified her conditions for redemption, which meant weeks of doing the things he hated more and things he enjoyed less. No progress report went unpunished, which seemed right since, according to her, he'd disappointed everyone possible, including God.

> "FOR MY THOUGHTS ARE NOT YOUR THOUGHTS, NEITHER ARE YOUR WAYS MY WAYS," DECLARES THE LORD. "AS THE HEAVENS ARE HIGHER THAN THE EARTH, SO ARE MY WAYS HIGHER THAN YOUR WAYS AND MY THOUGHTS THAN YOUR THOUGHTS."
>
> —Isaiah 55:8-9

Preachers are people who launch into sermons, regardless of the reason. They use condemning language with religious themes. Often, they use these sermons to pontificate on the faults of the person as well as the world in general. To a Preacher, even small sins have huge spiritual ramifications, usually ending in someone going to hell, either figuratively or literally. Preachers are all about fire and brimstone, religious Chicken Littles, for whom the spiritual sky is always falling. Because God is invoked, taking exception to the Preacher is like questioning God.

Preachers invoke God not to be instructive about his character or attributes but to coerce compliance with what they want. When God is continually presented as a vengeful and condemning judge, the fullness of his love and mercy are withheld, along with forgiveness and grace. Preachers believe they are standing in God's place when they are really usurping it.

THE ROLE REVERSER

"*This* isn't going to go well," I remember thinking to myself when this mom and dad brought their son in for counseling. The parents were divorced, and it was clear from their body language they still had unresolved issues. The dad, Brent, was the driver for counseling. The mom, Nancy, didn't seem to care if she didn't have to pay for it. The son, Andy, was just keeping his head down and out of the line of fire between his parents. The issue was Andy's grades (or lack thereof). If he didn't get a handle on his GPA, baseball next season was out, and Brent was an assistant coach for the team.

Andy seemed like a likeable kid. Fifteen is a tough age in general, but Andy was clearly miserable. When I asked him about the divorce, he said he was okay with it. He said he knew it had to happen but didn't say why.

I asked him about the custody arrangements. His parents lived less than ten minutes from each other, and he was always bouncing back and forth between them. It took me a while to figure out Andy felt abandoned by both.

Once the divorce happened, Andy stopped being a kid. Where his mother was concerned, he became more of her companion, her confidant. She poured out her feelings of loneliness to Andy, telling him she didn't know what she'd do without him. He had to listen as she railed against his father and was expected to choose sides. Andy was also expected to clean the apartment when she was too tired, which was often.

He found himself preparing more of the meals. On the weekends Andy was with her, he was expected to do the things she wanted or needed to do. Nancy complained if he wanted to spend time with friends, bemoaning the fact that everyone had abandoned her.

> WHEN I WAS A CHILD, I TALKED LIKE A CHILD, I THOUGHT LIKE A CHILD, I REASONED LIKE A CHILD. WHEN I BECAME A MAN, I PUT THE WAYS OF CHILDHOOD BEHIND ME.
>
> —1 Corinthians 13:11

It wasn't much better when Andy was with his father. Weekends at Brent's were one long party—eating pizza, watching sports and movies. That was great at first, but Brent didn't want to hear about the struggles Andy was having. Nothing negative got very far. Andy and Brent were supposed to be guys, just having fun. If something (besides girls) was bothering Andy, those issues were for when he was with his mom. Even the outside counseling was a way to get another adult to deal with Andy's issues.

Brent had turned Andy from a son into a buddy, treating him not as an adolescent but as a peer. But Andy didn't feel like a peer. He didn't need a buddy; he had friends at school. What he needed was a dad. Andy felt squeezed out between who Nancy and Brent wanted him to be. There seemed to be no time left for Andy to be who he was—a struggling, hurting fifteen-year-old boy.

There is a time and a place for a child to become a parental caregiver. This transition is a natural stage toward the end of life, not at the beginning. I heartily agree that children should learn how to handle responsibility, but I also believe that children should not be asked to shoulder adult responsibility. When parents expect children to function like adults, they rob those children of their childhood.

Forcing the transition to adulthood too early is emotionally abusive. The Bible talks about a time to move on from childish things, but this implies that there is a time for childish things. Kids need to be allowed to be kids.

THE HISTORIAN

Angela had been stewing for days in her own discontent. For some unknown reason, she'd gained weight. The work week had been especially frustrating, and now Ted was late getting back from fishing. Even though she said it was fine for him to be gone most of Saturday, she spent the whole day feeling sorry for herself and resenting his audacity at having fun while she was so miserable.

When he finally walked in the door, she yelled, "Get those muddy boots off my clean carpet!"

Ted jumped back onto the linoleum floor as if stung. Looking down at the carpet he'd just vacated, he said, "Come on, Angie! They're not that bad!" He started removing them anyway.

"I've spent the entire day cleaning and what do you care? You never care about the house!"

"Sure, I do! Look, is this about me going fishing? Because there are plenty of weekends when all I do is work in the yard. You never care about the yard!"

Angela couldn't believe he was trying to place blame on her when he should be sorry for tracking dirt into the house. "Of course I care about the yard," she snapped back defensively.

"Well, I always tell you how nice the house looks!"

"When's the last time you said anything about the house?" Angela demanded.

Ted looked blank for a second, then responded, "I can't remember the last time. That's not the point!" Grabbing up his boots, he made a beeline for the garage. Coming back through the laundry room a second later, he asked, "When's the last time you said anything about the yard?"

Angela felt victory at hand. "I said something about the yard twice in the past two weeks. A week ago, on Thursday when we were walking out the car, I mentioned how nice the lawn looked. And last weekend, I said something when you brought in those flowers." For a second, she felt a twinge of guilt at the way she was yelling at

> LOVE IS PATIENT, LOVE IS KIND. IT DOES NOT ENVY, IT DOES NOT BOAST, IT IS NOT PROUD. IT DOES NOT DISHONOR OTHERS, IT IS NOT SELF-SEEKING, IT IS NOT EASILY ANGERED, IT KEEPS NO RECORD OF WRONGS. LOVE DOES NOT DELIGHT IN EVIL BUT REJOICES WITH THE TRUTH.
>
> –1 Corinthians 13:4–6

Ted, remembering how cute he's been, bringing in the flowers in his water bottle. But this was no time to go soft. "I notice when you've done something nice. You could at least do the same for me!"

Ted opened his mouth to speak but just looked bewildered. She'd won. If it came down to a battle of details, Angela usually did. She could pull examples out of thin air. They were impossible to dispute because, after he cooled off and thought back, he'd eventually remember. He was never off the hook for any careless remark or thoughtless act. There was never a pardon or a reprieve. His guilt just kept being recycled, even from years past. He wondered how many times this argument would be thrown back in his face.

Historians are a repository of every bad thing they think you've ever said or done, real or imagined. The details of your failure are categorized and logged, ready to be brought up as evidence against you. Putting the past behind you is not an option for a Historian. The Historian always keeps your faults front and center to deflect attention away from their own faults.

This type of emotional abuse can be damaging because the Historian appears to be presenting facts. Places, times, dates, conversations—all these details lend weight to their conclusions. Because the details are accurate, their conclusions can seem accurate as well. And, because the role of Historian is to be the keeper of the "facts," the Historian usurps the interpretation of those "facts."

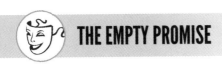

THE EMPTY PROMISE

Jenny knew asking her mother to drive her over to Becky's was a risk, but she didn't have another way to get there.

"Mom? Becky's having a bunch of friends over for a sleepover tonight. Could you take me over there later?" The problem wasn't about Becky or the sleepover; her mom knew the family. The problem was her mother.

"Why Becky? That's like, over an hour, to take you back and forth today and tomorrow. I've got stuff I've got to do this weekend. If you want me to take you then you're going to have to help me get my stuff done."

"Okay," Jenny agreed. "What do you need me to do?" She got her mom a piece of paper and a pencil so she could write down the additional chores she wanted done. Jenny took the finished list and got started, all while her mother continued to sit at the kitchen table, drinking coffee and reading the paper.

The chances of her mother taking her were, Jenny figured, thirty-seventy. She could get through the list and be ready to go, but her mother could find something else that had to be done or some other excuse not to make good on her promise. Asking her mom for anything was a risk.

In some ways, Jenny knew it would be easier to just be told "no." Whenever her mother said "yes," to one of her requests, hope was ignited. And, once that "yes" had been given, other pathways to getting what Jenny wanted were taken off the table. She was stuck with waiting to see if the "yes" might truly happen.

> DO I MAKE MY PLANS IN A WORLDLY MANNER SO THAT IN THE SAME BREATH I SAY BOTH "YES, YES" AND "NO, NO"? BUT AS SURELY AS GOD IS FAITHFUL, OUR MESSAGE TO YOU IS NOT "YES" AND "NO."
>
> –2 Corinthians 1:17b-18

An Empty Promise is a house of cards. It has the appearance of stability, but a puff of wind can cause collapse. People who are Empty Promisers say yes but then find reasons not to follow through. Those reasons, generally, are presented as not their fault so they don't accept responsibility. If you press an Empty Promise, you risk being blamed. The Empty Promise teaches that words and promises don't mean anything. And when words and promises don't mean anything, there is no security, no stability. Hope is ignited, then doused.

THE SILENT TREATMENT

The house was dark when Sarah arrived at home, but Carl's car was in the driveway. No lights on to welcome her home. "What have I done now?" she wondered. A darkened house with his car in the driveway meant that Carl had barricaded himself in the basement. He did that whenever he was mad about something or someone. The "what" didn't matter; the "who was to blame" would be her. It wasn't logical but it's the way he was.

Sarah pulled her car up next to his and let herself into the house as quietly as she could. She'd learned long ago that it was worse if she tried to find out what was wrong. Things were better if she just stayed out of his way and waited for him to tell her what she'd done wrong.

Depending upon how mad he was, he could keep this up for hours and even days. If she tried to talk to him, he'd walk away. He'd watch television late into the night and wait until she was asleep before coming up to bed. In the morning, he'd wait until she was in the shower to get up himself.

She'd learned Carl wasn't so much avoiding her as punishing her. The first few years of their marriage, Sarah had told him how much this behavior hurt her. She realized now she shouldn't have done that. The behavior had only gotten worse.

> A SOOTHING TONGUE
> IS A TREE OF LIFE,
> BUT A PERVERSE TONGUE
> CRUSHES THE SPIRIT.
>
> —Proverbs 15:4

At some point, he'd start talking to her again, if only to let her know how wrong she was about something, how it was her fault. She would need to apologize and promise not to do whatever it was again. But she knew her promises wouldn't make any difference, because he'd just find fault with something else.

In other aspects of her life, Sarah enjoyed the quiet. She liked reading in a quiet house with a cup of hot tea. She liked walking in her neighborhood without wires dangling out of her ears. But this quiet was different. This quiet wasn't peaceful. This quiet was angry; the brooding quiet of a storm about to hit.

We've looked at the damage of emotional abuse, often done with words. The Silent Treatment is emotionally abusive by the withholding of words of relationship.

The Silent Treatment comes with variations. Sometimes, the person refuses to speak to the other person. Other times, the person refuses to allow the other person to speak. Conversation is held captive. The person who engages in the silent treatment may physically withdraw from the other person or remain in proximity but hold him- or herself aloof and unapproachable. The message, however, is clear in all these forms—I refuse to interact with you because you are not worthy.

"*He* never wrote to me. He never called. He never sent a card on my birthday. It was like I didn't exist." She sounded wounded and incredulous. "How does someone do that?" This didn't seem the time to try to make excuses for an absent father. How could a father abandon his child? Yet, I'd heard the same lament multiple times from daughters and sons who had become invisible children.

Tracy originally came to work with me because her second marriage was in trouble. Tracy and Jason were arguing much of the time and she was scared. She wanted this marriage to work out for herself and for the kids.

"She keeps treating me like a child," Jason complained. "Always over-explaining everything. You should see the notes I get from her. She wants to know where I am every minute of the day. I don't know what she's afraid of. She sure doesn't trust me."

As I worked with Tracy on the source of her fear and distrust, we eventually arrived at her father's abandonment. Tracy learned at an early age that someone you loved could simply disappear from your life. Her mother, over the years, tried to console Tracy by saying things were better without him in their lives, but it took Tracy until she was a teenager to scab over that emotional wound. She decided she wasn't going to be hurt like that again. Then, she was. Her first marriage lasted less than two years.

When she got married to Jason, she was determined to stay firmly in control. At first, Jason liked that she was so attentive to their relationship. As time went on, however, he began to doubt her attentiveness was about him and began to suspect it was more about her. He felt suffocated by her need to be in control of his life.

> THE LORD HIMSELF GOES BEFORE YOU AND WILL BE WITH YOU; HE WILL NEVER LEAVE YOU NOR FORSAKE YOU. DO NOT BE AFRAID; DO NOT BE DISCOURAGED.
>
> —Deuteronomy 31:8

M.I.A.—missing in action. Gone but not forgotten. Watched for but not seen. No calls. No cards. No visits. How do you handle it when someone you love moves on and you're the one left behind? I've heard it described as being a scrap of paper, discarded like litter and left to blow in the wind.

The M.I.A. Parent is a tragic form of emotional abuse. In other forms, the emotional abuse is carried out through the presence of words and actions. For the M.I.A. Parent, the emotional abuse is carried out through the absence of words and actions. And that absence can speak louder than words. Tracy needed to understand Jason wasn't her father, and for the good of their marriage, she needed to stop treating him as if he was.

Abandonment is a deep-seated fear. It is the panic of an infant who loses sight of the parent. Of a child who looks up in a crowded store and sees no one familiar. Praise God, our heavenly Father, for understanding and addressing this fear.

Understand *the* Past—Unlock *the* Future

Almost everyone I've worked with on uncovering and healing from emotional abuse will, at some point in the process, ask why they have to go through the pain all over again. Feeling pain to heal from pain seems counterintuitive. Yet, emotional abuse needs to be uncovered and confronted, even if it was years in the past. Those patterns of abuse can negatively affect the present and, if untreated, the future. Emotional abuse doesn't stay in the past. Instead, emotional abuse leads to:

▨ LOW SELF-ESTEEM

Automatically devaluing your own thoughts and opinions and elevating the thoughts and opinions of others

▨ LACK OF SELF-CONFIDENCE

Difficulty making decisions, second-guessing decisions you've made, seeking situations that don't threaten your low opinion of your abilities

▨ TRANSFER OF NEEDS

Finding comfort and solace for the pain in addictive behaviors

ACTING OUT SEXUALLY

Using sexuality to seek comfort and meet needs

LONELINESS

The inability to establish meaningful connections with others, including yourself

FAILURE SYNDROME

A deep-seated fear that you aren't worthy of good things in your life, so you make sure they don't happen

PERFECTIONISM

An obsessive preoccupation with doing everything "right" in order to deserve love and affirmation

UNREALISTIC GUILT

Believing anything wrong that happens around you is your fault

CRISIS-ORIENTED

Believing your "job" is to fix whatever is wrong and your only value is when you are working hard to do so

UNRESOLVED ANGER AND RESENTMENT

Anger at the injustice and pain can go unresolved, building up year after year, relationship after relationship

Emotional abuse is like the thief Jesus talks about, who comes to steal (your sense of self), kill (your joy in life) and destroy (your relationships). Jesus said this isn't the life he wants for you, "I have come that they may have life, and have it to the full" (John 10:10b). Emotional abuse seeks to limit your choices, your value, and your worth. Healing from emotional abuse gives you the opportunity to regain a full and healthier life.

FEELING PAIN TO HEAL FROM PAIN SEEMS COUNTERINTUITIVE.

Steps *to* Healing

The message of emotional abuse is often "You never do anything right." The reverberations of this message may cause you to set the bar too high on what counts as progress in recovering from the effects of emotional abuse. Healing isn't a task you have to be perfect at, nor a race that only has one finish line. Healing is a process. You know this from physical healing. A person who has broken a leg isn't expected to walk overnight, even with a cast. Emotional injuries can be like physical injuries; they take time to heal. With that in mind, here are ten steps to healing from emotional abuse to help guide you through the process.

■ ■ ■

Step 1: Moving Beyond Blame

When the truth of emotional abuse finally comes out, it hurts. And when we hurt, we search for the reason; we look for someone to blame. Some people I've worked with were the victims of truly evil people who took pleasure in creating pain for others. However, most people were emotionally abused by someone who meant better than what they did, tried less than they should, or who chose not to know better.

Sometimes, an emotionally abusive pattern is perpetuated because those are the behaviors the abuser knows. Other times, it occurs because the abuser is simply weak. They know they should act and speak differently but they don't have the strength, courage, or motivation to do so. When you are in relationship with these types of people, you desperately want them to overcome their weakness so they can love you like they should. But they don't and that hurts.

> DISCRETION WILL PROTECT YOU, AND UNDERSTANDING WILL GUARD YOU.
>
> —Proverbs 2:11

When we're in pain, we seek to know why, what, and who is responsible. I've found when a person who has suffered emotional abuse works through the temptation to blame him- or herself, the next stop on the blame train is the abuser. Understanding why, what, and who is responsible for emotional abuse is a valuable destination. Staying stuck in blame is not.

The truly evil person is immune to blame. The weak person is often blind to it. Sometimes the person to "blame" is dead, and vindication is not possible. Blame doesn't stick. These situations leave the person who is recovering from emotional abuse unsatisfied and empty.

Instead of seeking blame, I encourage people to seek understanding. If your abuser is truly evil, then you are not to blame. You can move on from that relationship. If your abuser acted out of faulty parenting patterns, you can come to understand such lack of awareness. If your abuser was tired, overwhelmed, stressed, distracted, or moody, then you can understand their weakness. Understanding can shift the causes of the emotional abuse away from you and onto the other person without leaving you stuck in a toxic pool of blame. Blame continues to fan the fires of anger, bitterness, and resentment, but too often you're the one burned. Understanding can provide you with a protective barrier of insight.

1. Fold a piece of paper in two lengthwise. On the left side, write down a short description of the wrongs done to you by an abuser. On the right side, write down any extenuating circumstances or situations that might have contributed to those actions.

Step 2: Granting Forgiveness

An emotional abuser seeks to crush your spirit so you will be more compliant and easier to control. Once that control is established, it is difficult to loosen the grip. This leash of control transcends decades, even reaching out from the grave.

Pamela came to me after battling for years with depression and anxiety. Upon the death of her mother, though, her symptoms worsened. Getting out of bed in the morning was a struggle. She had to take a leave of absence from work because she couldn't concentrate. Her world seemed to be falling apart and she couldn't understand why it was happening now.

Pamela thought that when her mother died, she'd finally be "free." The relationship between them had been difficult from the very beginning. Her mother was constantly putting her down, criticizing her for the way she lived, the way she looked, the decisions she made, and the outcomes those decisions produced.

Pamela never did anything right, even after she moved in with her aging mother. Pamela thought she might be able to repair the relationship if she did the "right" thing and took care of her mother. Instead, the relationship seemed to get worse the older her mother got. Pamela was there right up to the end, waiting for her mother to ask forgiveness and say she loved her. "And that never happened," she told me.

FORGIVING SOMEONE DOES NOT MEAN FORGETTING WHAT THAT PERSON DID. FORGIVENESS SHOWS YOUR WILLINGNESS TO CREATE THE POSSIBILITY OF A FRESH START.

"If she'd asked for forgiveness before she died, what would you have done?" I asked. Pamela thought for a minute, teared up, and said, "I would have forgiven her. I wanted to forgive her, but she didn't ask and now it's too late."

"Why is it too late? Can't you still forgive her?"

"What good would that do?" she asked, clearly irritated. "She's dead! She'd never know!"

"True," I conceded, "but you would."

So often, people think that forgiveness is a gift given only to the person who did wrong. But, forgiveness is also a gift to the person who was wronged. When you say, "I forgive you," what you are saying is, "I acknowledge you wronged me and need forgiveness. I choose to forgive you and, by doing so, I take back control over my part of our relationship."

When you fail to grant forgiveness, you chain yourself to that act or pattern of pain. You allow that pain to continue to hurt you. I've known people who spent decades of their lives angry and bitter over wrongs done to them in the past. In many cases, the person who intentionally or even inadvertently hurt them moved on with their lives and the only one still stuck was the victim.

> BEAR WITH EACH OTHER AND FORGIVE ONE ANOTHER IF ANY OF YOU HAS A GRIEVANCE AGAINST SOMEONE. FORGIVE AS THE LORD FORGAVE YOU.
>
> —Colossians 3:13

Forgiving someone does not mean forgetting what that person did. Forgiveness shows your willingness to create the possibility of a fresh start. As Jesus said, "If your brother or sister sins, go and point out their fault, just between the two of you. If they listen to you, you have won them over" (Matthew 18:15).

If they don't listen to you, you can still know that the Lord has heard you. God is in the forgiveness business, which is a good thing considering we are the ones he forgives. Because God forgives us, he expects us to forgive others. In the Lord's Prayer, Jesus establishes a standard of forgiveness, and that standard is how well we forgive others.[4]

As people, we want retribution. God, however, desires repentance. Forgiveness doesn't guarantee repentance, but it certainly opens the door wider for repentance. When we forgive and that person responds, we win that person over. If the person is unreceptive, God tells us to move on and leave vengeance to him.[5]

ACTION STEPS:

1. Using your list, write a letter to your abuser, acknowledging the pain and expressing as much forgiveness as you can.

2. If you're able, send the letter to your abuser.

3 If you're not able, "give" your letter to God by putting it in a "God Box," or burning it as a sacrifice, asking God for strength to forgive.

Step 3: Reclaiming Personal Power

Emotional abuse is a practice designed to convince you with words, actions, and ideas that you are powerless and without rights. This is a lie; you have both rights and power. You have the right not to be emotionally abused. You have the power to say no if someone threatens to hurt you. You have the right to get on with your life free from abusive relationships. You have the power to forgive those who hurt you.

> EACH ONE SHOULD TEST THEIR OWN ACTIONS. THEN THEY CAN TAKE PRIDE IN THEMSELVES ALONE, WITHOUT COMPARING THEMSELVES TO SOMEONE ELSE, FOR EACH ONE SHOULD CARRY THEIR OWN LOAD.
>
> —Galatians 6:4–5

You have a right to make your own decisions, even if those differ from the decisions of others. If you've suffered with emotional abuse, you may doubt your ability to make good decisions. Reclaiming your personal power means learning to love and trust yourself. I know a man who went back to school and began a second career, realizing his first career had been his father's decision, not his. Then there was the woman who rearranged and redecorated her house, realizing she'd chosen items and colors her mother liked and approved, but she really didn't like them. I've seen people change their style of dress, their style of hair, or where they lived as statements of independence and reconnection with their personal power. In each case, they battled fear yet experienced exhilaration at connecting with themselves instead of trying to be or please someone else.

YOU HAVE THE RIGHT NOT TO BE EMOTIONALLY ABUSED.

Reclaiming your personal power, however, isn't just finding a way to say "yes" to the things you really want. It is also finding a way to say "no" to the things other people really want from or for you, even if those things are good. Many emotional abusers will try to force you into a black-and-white world of stark decisions, where their opinion is "great" and yours is "horrible." A great many decisions in life aren't between the great and the horrible; they lie somewhere in between. Don't fall for that trap!

Ultimately, you are responsible for your own choices and actions.

ACTION STEPS:

1. Find a quiet place where you won't be disturbed or distracted.

2. Write down everything that is good about you. If you have difficulty starting the list, begin with this fundamental truth: I am a child of God.

3. Pray for God to speak into your heart all the good things he sees and knows about you.

4. Use what you learn about yourself to help inform your choices and decisions going forward, becoming even more who God knows you can be.

Step 4: Avoiding Conflicts

Being in relationship with an emotionally abusive person means you are constantly engaged in a battle of wills at some level. These battles invariably involve conflict. For the most severely abusive people, the only way to avoid conflict may be to exit the relationship completely. Emotionally abusive people are toxic; they poison relationships with their need for control, their negativity, and their lack of respect. Limiting contact can reduce your toxic exposure.

Often the relationships that cause the most tension are in the family—parent to child, child to parent, sibling to sibling. What do you do when contact happens at events like family gatherings, weddings, birthdays, and holidays? I suggest that you designate a trusted individual to act as an emotional buffer. An emotional buffer is someone who understands the dynamics of the relationship and agrees to step in to offer support in certain circumstances.

> IF IT IS POSSIBLE, AS FAR AS IT DEPENDS ON YOU, LIVE AT PEACE WITH EVERYONE.
>
> —Romans 12:18

One young woman I know decided to confront her father's persistent negativity toward her. As her children became older, she did not want them exposed to his dismissive and disrespectful pattern of speaking to her. She felt ready to be honest about how his words and actions made her feel, but she was still terrified.

In talking with her husband, I suggested he be present when she spoke with her father, to act as that emotional buffer. I cautioned him not to feel like it was his job to "rescue" her. Instead, they came up with parameters for when and how he would interject himself into her conversation with her father. If her father began to raise his voice, her husband would repeat the father's name quietly. If she became emotionally overwhelmed, her husband would paraphrase her last comments, to give her time to compose herself. If her father rejected her perception of how he treated her, her husband would calmly provide several examples he had witnessed.

EMOTIONALLY ABUSIVE PEOPLE ARE TOXIC.

Another way to shield yourself from potential conflicts is by calling on the phone, sending cards, or meeting in public places. Another woman made it a habit to meet her mother at various museums or art galleries around town, which she knew her mother would enjoy, due to a lifelong interest in art. This woman also intentionally guided the conversation to what her mother thought about the exhibits, not because she didn't have an opinion herself but so their time together would be more positive. She wanted to spend time with her mother and sought ways to reduce the conflict when possible. Of course, it wasn't always possible, but often it was, and that was enough for her.

Being intentional about reducing conflicts is not capitulating or giving in. Rather, it is proactively managing the relationship and protecting your boundaries. In this way, you show love and affection to the other person without sacrificing yourself.

ACTION STEPS:

1. Identify the toxic people in your life.

2. Identify people in your life who can act as an emotional buffer for you in difficult situations.

3. Speak to those individuals, explain what they mean to you, and request that they support you, when asked, in this capacity.

Step 5: Addressing Hurts

Understanding and forgiving wounds from your past will not keep you from being hurt in the present or the future. If you have been emotionally abused, you will want to develop different and healthier ways of dealing with pain than what you've done previously.

1. When dealing with an offense, keep the offense in the present, not in the past. A harsh comment by a coworker today is not a validation of harsh comments experienced in your past. That coworker doesn't know about your past and is not intentionally trying to add to it. Maybe he had a bad day. Maybe she's worried about something that has nothing to do with you. Learn to separate what is happening now from what happened then.

2. Resist reacting with hostility. If someone does or says something that hurts you, explain how you felt. Reacting with hostility not only escalates the conflict but can compromise your ability to remain in control of yourself.

3. Give up the need to be right. I know how hard this one is, but other people are entitled to their own thoughts and opinions. You may view something they did as hurtful, but they may not. When differences of opinion arise, recognize the most you may achieve is an agreement to disagree.

4. Take responsibility for yourself. You oversee your own thoughts and actions. Avoid the temptation of blaming others for "making" you do something. Part of reclaiming your personal power is understanding that it includes

the power to make your own decisions, even your own mistakes.

5 Respond instead of reacting. Reactions tend to be immediate and on "autopilot." Emotional abuse may have made your autopilot extremely sensitive. If you feel yourself immediately reacting, slow down, take a deep breath, say a prayer, or recite a saying or verse. You can think before you act—that is the essence of intentional response.

6 Try to build a bridge, not burn one. When I was growing up, this concept was encapsulated in the phrase "the benefit of the doubt." Even though you may be hurt or dismayed by what the person said or did, you can still respond to that person, at the least, in a polite manner. This way, you will be able to gauge if what you experienced was a mistake or a misunderstanding. Be open to the possibility you misunderstood and seek to clarify their intent.

7 Recognize the difference between the target and the source. Some people, when they are angry, spread that anger out at everyone and everything they can find. You may be the target of that anger, but you are not the source. The patterns of emotional abuse can make you take on undeserved responsibility. Be alert so that you don't accept false guilt from others.

8 Know your limits. You have a right to set personal boundaries and to limit what you will accept from others. You have a right to communicate those boundaries and expect them to be respected. You have a right to those limits even in the face of opposition.

9 Retain your personal happiness. If someone hurts you, this doesn't mean you must give over your personal happiness. If the hurt was unintentional, you can use this as a reminder that people make mistakes, including yourself. If the hurt was intentional, you can limit future dealings with this person. Either way, why hang on to the hurt? Fretting about it and replaying it in your mind, remembering how much it hurt, will only hurt you again. Why do that to yourself? Don't use someone else's hurtful action to bash yourself.

Step 6: Maintaining Healthy Relationships

To maintain a healthy relationship, you need to have one in the first place. If you've suffered from emotional abuse, you've experienced a negative and hurtful relationship. You may, because that relationship was presented as normal, seek out similar "normal" relationships. For example, children told they were worthless or unlovable may find adult partners who agree with that assessment. Children who spent years striving to please an unresponsive parent may seek out unresponsive adults, thinking that this time will be different. Children who learned to live at arm's length from others out of distrust may become emotionally distant and guarded adults.

How are your current relationships? If you looked at each, which would you consider positive and beneficial? Which ones cause you to feel fearful, nervous, or unsure? When healing from emotional abuse, there is generally a pivotal, primary abusive relationship that stands out. However, there is value in evaluating all relationships, not just the obvious one, to determine how that relationship may have affected or influenced other relationships. You may discover you've brought a father into your marriage or a mother into your friendships. Perhaps you brought a brother or sister into your workplace. Or, maybe you've become someone you said you would never be like to your children. The tendrils of emotional abuse can be long, binding past to present with unintended consequences.

THE BEST WAY TO MAINTAIN A HEALTHY RELATIONSHIP IS TO BECOME HEALTHY YOURSELF.

The best way to maintain a healthy relationship is to become healthy yourself. Consider that the relationship you need to spend the most time and energy on is the one you have with yourself. Healthy people tend to attract healthy people.

If you didn't grow up with good examples of healthy relationships, you can still learn what they are. Pay attention to the relationships other people have. Watch friends and acquaintances interact with each other. Look for those who exhibit the fruit of God's Spirit— love, joy, peace, forbearance, kindness, goodness, faithfulness, gentleness, and self-control.[6] These are the relationships and the people you want to learn from. Ask questions. Seek guidance. Find out how they're able to put these attributes into living, breathing action. Then, choose one fruit of the Spirit to practice. Try it first with yourself and then with others.

Love and find joy in who you are, live at peace with yourself, exercise restraint when dealing with yourself, be kind to yourself, know God made you good, be faithful to the best of who you are, treat yourself gently, and give yourself the gift of self-control. When you can treat yourself this way, you will be able to recognize these traits in others. You will be able to give others the same gifts you give to yourself.

1. Write down each significant relationship you have, even if the other person is no longer actively in relationship with you.

2. Take time to evaluate each relationship—what positives you gained and what negatives you endured.

3. Determine which relationships you should hold on to and which relationships you need to begin to let go, for your own healing.

4. Commit to spending time each week concentrating on your relationship with yourself by engaging in a personally refreshing activity.

5. Commit to enhancing your spiritual relationship by establishing a quiet time for prayer and reflection.

Step 7: Healthy Communication

Because so much of emotional abuse has to do with how one person communicates with another, please consider incorporating these steps into your relationships to help develop healthy communication.

1. Approach others with gentleness and openness. This can be difficult because of a fear of hostility or rejection. However, trying to shield yourself through cynicism, sarcasm, and even undue deference does not set the stage for healthy communication. Instead, take the risk and start with honesty. You will know, soon enough, if the other person is responding with gentleness and openness back. Better to know that sooner rather than later.

2. Don't assume you know everything. You may understand certain facts and be familiar with how you view a situation, but you can't know what the other person knows or feels until you ask.

3. Speak what you know. Don't be afraid to give your opinion and perspective or communicate the facts, as you know them. Speak out confidently but without a desire to harm the other person. Truth shouldn't be used as a bludgeon to batter and separate people. Truth should be used to bring people together.

4. Manage your emotions. I'm not saying you should deny your emotions when communicating with others, but I do think you should manage them. Unchecked emotions

can spin out of control, causing damage. Unchecked emotions can also overshadow the message you're trying to get across.

(5) Be aware of different communication styles. Different people often communicate differently, so take that into account. If the conversation is not demeaning or belittling, try to focus on *what* is being said instead of *how* it's being said. Ask questions and respond in the communication style that works best for you. Even if the other person is a bit blunt or provides more explanation than you like, you can still have a meaningful, respectful conversation.

(6) Allow other opinions. A conversation is a success not if both sides agree with each other but if both sides understand each other. Just because a person holds a different opinion from you doesn't mean one of you is wrong. An opinion is just that—an opinion, which comes from different experiences and perspectives. You should not be surprised or threatened if a person different from you holds a different opinion.

(7) Seek common ground. When differences of opinion arise, work to communicate acceptance without agreement. Acceptance of the person in the face of disagreement allows for the relationship to continue.

8 Watch your motives. Avoid entering into communication with others when you're angry or tired or restless or upset. Sadly, we can use others as verbal punching bags when we're ready for a fight. Especially for difficult topics or when you feel emotionally volatile, be very sure what, why, and how you're communicating. When in doubt (and even when you're not), pray first and ask God for wisdom.

9 Allow other conclusions. People need the freedom to make their own choices, even if you disagree. If those choices cause you pain, you can let the person know.

10 Use "I" not "you." Focus your side of the communication on what you are feeling and thinking. Avoid the temptation of assigning thoughts and motives to the other person. Speak for yourself and let the other person do likewise.

11 Exercise forgiveness. People make mistakes, including you. If you make a mistake, admit it and ask for forgiveness. If the other person makes a mistake, acknowledge it and grant forgiveness.

12 Do what you say. If you say you'll do something, do it. Do it in the way you said it, in the time frame given, for the reasons presented, and in the manner you outlined. Live truthfully. When you act with integrity, you build trust. Trust is essential to healthy communication. After all, why should I talk to you if I can't believe what you say?

Step 8: Discovering Gifts *and* Talents

Emotional abuse seeks to rob you of a sense of self, so you are easier to manipulate and control. Because of this, you may have learned not to trust yourself or consider yourself valuable or worthwhile. When asked what your gifts and talents are, you may automatically assume that you have none.

I've always liked this verse from the Old Testament—"Each of you must bring a gift in proportion to the way the LORD your God has blessed you" (Deuteronomy 16:17). Of course, I recognize the context here is offering sacrifices, but I think it transcends sheep or goats, rams or doves. What I get from this statement is that each person does have a gift. Why would God say you "must" bring something you don't have? The verse also says that the gift you offer comes from what God has already provided.

YOU HAVE A GIFT TO OFFER GOD. THERE IS NO ONE ELSE IN THE ENTIRE WORLD JUST LIKE YOU.

You have a gift to offer God. This gift comes from what God has already blessed you with. And what God has blessed you with is your uniqueness. There is no one else in the entire world just like you. I would like you to consider that, instead of thinking you have no gifts or talents, you may not know what they are. You may have discovered one or some of those gifts, but there may be more waiting to be explored.

In order to discover your gifts and talents, you may need to turn off the old messages of worthlessness and imperfection. These messages tell you there's nothing to find, so why even search? Instead, you should listen to what God has to say about who you are. He gave you your gifts so you could use them for your good and for the good of others, all to his glory. Those gifts are there, even if you can't see them now. If you can't find them, ask God what they are. Jesus said, "For everyone who asks receives; the one who seeks finds; and to the one who knocks, the door will be opened" (Luke 11:10).

God has a track record of empowering unlikely people to do extraordinary things. But remember, God may have a different definition from you of extraordinary. He doesn't always go for bells and whistles. Jesus pointed to small children and said the kingdom of heaven belonged to them.[7] He also said that greatness was found in servanthood.[8] When looking for gifts and talents, I suggest you use the eyes of God to point you in the right direction. Otherwise, you might walk right on past one without noticing.

ACTION STEPS:

1 Don't know your gifts or talents? Think back to what you enjoyed doing as a child, before other people stepped in and created doubt. Make a list of those things and find ways to incorporate them into your life.

2 Register for a class at a college or community center.

3 Identify five things you have always been interested in doing and make a plan to do at least two of them. Take a risk and try something new.

4 Talk to trusted family or friends and ask them what they notice about you, what you're good at, or what you're naturally able to do. Ask God to reveal the gifts he's given you and then be prepared for surprises. Each day pray this prayer: *Dear Father, show me the gifts you've already given me so I can give to others and give you glory.*

Step 9: Solving Problems

To help you on this journey of healing, I've developed a list of characteristics of healthy problem-solvers. Problems carry with them the seeds of both consensus and conflict. Those who have had their self-esteem battered by emotional abuse can have difficulty dealing with problems because of the potential for conflict. Either they refuse to stand their ground and give in, or they turn every conflict into a do-or-die battleground of "This time I'll win!" There is a middle ground between these two extremes. Granted, this middle ground takes more time to accomplish, but it has the best chance of allowing both parties to remain standing at the end.

ACTION STEPS:

1 Resolve to solve the problem, not to win. If you only want to "win," you may find that you've won the battle but lost the war. Problems and how they are handled have short-term and long-term consequences. Be aware of both. Consider a strategy, not a battle plan.

2 Face the problem. Plan a specific time for a conversation to identify the areas of concern and be prepared to offer options for solution. Some problems won't go away on their own. For those that won't, I suggest facing them instead of avoiding them. As soon as possible, find a way to deal with the problem. Those left unattended can balloon out of control and are harder to address later.

3 Be open to unique solutions. Usually, when I perceive a problem, I have an initial idea of how to solve it. Sometimes, though, once I hear different opinions, I change my mind on how to deal with the problem. I may have a good solution, but I may not have the best solution.

4 Be clear on your boundaries. People can become emotionally heated when working through problems. Know your limits. Know what behaviors you are not willing to accept from others, or from yourself.

5 Forgive yourself and others. When the boundaries are breached, repair them with forgiveness.

6 Accept that life is not always fair. Problems, and the way people handle them, do not always seem fair. What is fair to one person may appear unfair to another.

7 Deal with one problem at a time. There may be other problems swirling around, but you can realistically only handle one at a time. Don't try to take on the problems of the world all at once.

8 Anticipate a positive outcome. When you enter problem-solving mode, be optimistic. This attitude may seem simplistic, but it is enormously helpful. If you begin to tackle a problem thinking there is no good answer, how motivated are you to solve it?

(9) Believe in your ability to solve the problem. This concept goes together with the one above but is a bit different. There is a difference between believing there is no answer and believing *you* have no answer. Trust yourself to be able to find a solution.

(10) When working through problems, be aware of how you're communicating to yourself and to others. Problems are stressful, so avoid autopilot problem-solving. Keep your head in the game and be aware of how everyone involved is dealing with the problem.

Step 10: Recognizing Progress

How do you arrive at the final step to recovery? Review and recognize the progress you've made on the other nine steps:

▪ *Step 1:* Moving Beyond Blame

▪ *Step 2:* Granting Forgiveness

▪ *Step 3:* Reclaiming Personal Power

▪ *Step 4:* Avoiding Conflicts

- *Step 5:* Addressing Hurts

- *Step 6:* Maintaining Healthy Relationships

- *Step 7:* Healthy Communication

- *Step 8:* Discovering Gifts and Talents

- *Step 9:* Solving Problems

Moving beyond the past and recapturing the present takes time and requires being intentional about the journey. During this process, you may doubt you'll ever get to your destination. Recognizing your progress is an important final step, one that gives you momentum to keep moving forward toward healing.

So, how do you know you're getting better? If you were healing from a physical injury, you could see the wound scab over and start to fill in. You could feel the itch of new tissue forming. Similarly, there are markers to healing from emotional abuse. These markers can sometimes occur in large, take-notice ways, but more often I've found them present in the small victories that people experience day by day.

I like to call these baby steps. They happen step by wobbly step. They happen amid two steps forward and one step back. They happen when you pull yourself up after landing on your backside. Don't overlook, dismiss, or despise them for being too small; they're meant to be small. They may be small, but they are progress. With each step, you're getting stronger and learning more.

Learn to watch for these baby steps to recovery in your everyday actions and attitudes:

- I'm finding more joy in life
- I'm learning to love and care for myself
- I smile more easily
- I'm learning to forgive myself
- I'm not so angry all the time
- I find I can laugh more easily
- I'm trusting myself more
- I'm trying new things
- I'm not isolating myself as much
- I'm learning to recognize and release false guilt
- I'm more comfortable with my own silence and the silence of others
- I'm learning to accept who I am in the moment
- I'm fighting fewer battles

- I'm more comfortable saying "no" to bad things

- I'm learning to say "no" even to good things, when those good things aren't right for me

- I'm learning to save "yes" for better things

- I'm holding on to hope

I believe in the power of God to do remarkable things in your life. God peopled an entire race from an elderly couple named Abraham and Sarah.[9] He called a prophet named John out of the womb.[10] He saved his people through an octogenarian named Moses[11] and sent his message through a youngster named Timothy.[12] God does not look at your outsides but at your insides.[13] There is still time for healing, for the promised abundant life.

HEALING ISN'T A TASK YOU HAVE TO BE PERFECT AT, NOR A RACE THAT ONLY HAS ONE FINISH LINE. HEALING IS A PROCESS.

God is not through with you. You continue to be his "work in progress." One of the most compelling ways you can show the power of God is through a healed life. You become a testimony to the miracle of restoration through faith, hope, and love.

My prayer for you is that you will continue your journey of healing from emotional abuse, tucked securely in the arms of God.

May you become the strong, resilient person God is able to make you through the things you have suffered, and may your suffering lead you to compassion and empathy amid the pain in this world.

May you hold on to the hope of God and keep the assurance of his unfailing love close to your heart as an anchor in this turbulent world.

Notes

1. John 8:32.

2. Philippians 4:7.

3. Genesis 25-28.

4. Matthew 6:12.

5. Romans 12:19.

6. Galatians 5:22-23.

7. Mark 10:14.

8. Matthew 23:11.

9. Genesis 18:11.

10. Luke 1:13-17.

11. Exodus 7:7.

12. 1 Timothy 4:1.

13. 1 Samuel 16:7.